AF584691

Artist's Studio

Sculpture

by Jenny Fretland VanVoorst

Bullfrog Books

Ideas for Parents and Teachers

Bullfrog Books let children practice reading informational text at the earliest reading levels. Repetition, familiar words, and photo labels support early readers.

Before Reading

- Discuss the cover photo. What does it tell them?
- Look at the picture glossary together. Read and discuss the words.

Read the Book

- "Walk" through the book and look at the photos. Let the child ask questions. Point out the photo labels.
- Read the book to the child, or have him or her read independently.

After Reading

- Prompt the child to think more. Ask: Have you ever made a figure out of clay? What did you make?

Bullfrog Books are published by Jump!
5357 Penn Avenue South
Minneapolis, MN 55419
www.jumplibrary.com

Library of Congress Cataloging-in-Publication Data

Fretland VanVoorst, Jenny, 1972–
Sculpture / by Jenny Fretland VanVoorst.
pages cm. — (Artist's studio)
Includes index.
ISBN 978-1-62031-284-1 (hardcover: alk. paper) —
ISBN 978-1-62496-344-5 (ebook)
1. Sculpture—Juvenile literature. I. Title.
NB1143.F74 2015
730—dc23
2015021767

Series Designer: Ellen Huber
Book Designer: Michelle Sonnek
Photo Researcher: Michelle Sonnek

Photo Credits: All photos by Shutterstock except: 123RF, 17; Adobe Stock, 15; Alamy, cover, 5; Dreamstime, 10, 16–17; Getty, 8–9, 22br; iStock, 6–7; neelsky/Shutterstock.com, 11; Thinkstock, 24; ZUMA Press, Inc./Alamy Stock Photo, 12–13.

Printed in the United States of America at Corporate Graphics in North Mankato, Minnesota.

Table of Contents

Let's Carve!

Rae is a sculptor.
She makes things out of clay.

She starts with a big lump.
What will she make? Let's see.

She adds clay here.

She removes clay there.

She uses tools.

She uses her hands, too.

Look!

It is a man.

Rae paints it with glaze.
Then she bakes it. All done.

Ty is a sculptor, too.
He carves stone.

He picks a piece.
It is hard.

First he shapes the rock.
He uses a hammer.
He uses a chisel.

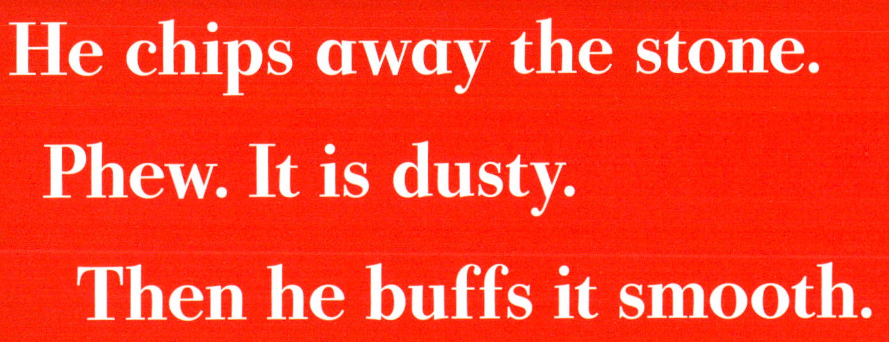

He chips away the stone.

Phew. It is dusty.

Then he buffs it smooth.

Look!

It is a rabbit.

Grab some clay.

Try it yourself!

Sculpting is fun.

Inside the Sculptor's Studio

Picture Glossary

buff
To rub or polish.

dusty
Filled with fine, dry, powdery particles.

chisel
A metal tool with a cutting edge used to shape or chip.

glaze
A glassy surface or coating.

Index

To Learn More

Learning more is as easy as 1, 2, 3.

1) Go to www.factsurfer.com

2) Enter "sculpture" into the search box.

3) Click the "Surf" button to see a list of websites.

With factsurfer.com, finding more information is just a click away.